STRUNG OUT ALONG THE ENDLESS BRANCH

Winner of the
2024 James Baker Hall Book Award

Strung Out Along the Endless Branch

by
Wesley Houp

Accents Publishing • Lexington, Kentucky • 2025

Printed in the United States of America

Accents Publishing
Editor: Katerina Stoykova
Cover Image: James Baker Hall

Library of Congress Control Number: 2025935409
ISBN: 978-1-961127-14-2
First Edition

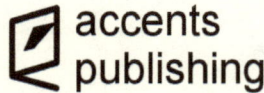

Accents Publishing is an independent press for brilliant voices. For a catalog of current and upcoming titles, please visit us on the Web at

www.accents-publishing.com

CONTENTS

I.

II.

I.

FALL MORNING

The school bus winds down
Laura Thompson Trail
plucking up the forest children
and trundling them off
to school in town
like a sack of acorns.
Sherry watches her
granddaughter lumber
up the narrow steps
beneath a bedazzled
backpack. I wave.
Sherry waves back,
a cup of coffee in her hand.
Two guineas cross the road.
There is no hurry in the
quiet despair of guineas.

THE ADVICE OF GOATS

She was cast as a villager
in the school play.
A minor role.
The teacher knew she was
a villager in real life
and that she'd muddle through.
At home she fed the guineas.
She fed the goat
who told her to unleash
herself.
Present your true self
like a howl,
like a pack of coyotes.

What the world fears most
is the advice of goats.

A HOLD

The sixth graders
at the old Liberty schoolhouse
skip reading lesson
to patch holes in
the rotten roof.
The bell rings for recess
in 1952, and no one
comes back for lunch.
James dresses up
in a flag-draped casket
from Vietnam.
Bill burns in his dad's barn.
Rita makes a mess of life
with white liquor,
and nobody says words
over little Carl after he
splits the atoms in his head.
So they line up buckets
to catch the rain.
Where's Ms. Jenkins?
they wonder aloud.
I'm right here, dears,
under the floor
with my Virginia Woolf.
Reach down and
grab a hold.

YOU MIGHT BE THE NEXT JONI MITCHELL

The first hard freeze
of October,

and all the best singers
are still women.

The children on
Simmons Bluff guard

the bus stop with
hoarfrost screams.

An eighth grader sleeps
in a crash of hormones.

A ballast of backpack
defies gravity.

The little girl from Alsup Mill
dances inside her shoes.

They arrested her mother
last night for possession.

All the Halloween lights
are blue, she tells a crow.

Ask Santa for a guitar
this year, he says.

Tell the grandma guinea
how you feel.

And when you get home
from school,

skip to the last page
before you run in the forest to cry.

ART CONTEST

Jacobi and Malachi
stole all the pencils
in the art room.

Not a single child
could find
a vanishing point.

The teacher
improvised a contest
from nothing.

The girl
in the back won
with her portrait

of a dead father
drawn lithely
in thin air.

She held
her finger up
to his mouth

a moment longer
to keep him
from apologizing.

INFINITY GIRL

The United Methodists
of Cainsville go in and out

side doors between sanctuary
and kitchen like orchard bees.

Happy, they do not smile trivially
but with genuine commitment

to preparation of beans, potatoes.
They give the children plenty

of rope, and the lanky blonde
girl in flip flops pulls hard.

It's not enough she tells
her mother. More.

She is supersonic on the swing set.
A solo mission to Mars.

Between gravity and the work
of knees, she's kindling the skill of

infinity. The sad weight
of everything lost—

the baby brother, the puppy
named Rigel, the blue ribbon piglet

that died of brucellosis—
only increases her speed,

her desire to let go,
eyes closed, and fold back

into her own wake,
a circuit of momentum

as harmless as a small body of light
that illuminates the playground.

PARCEL POST

From the corner of my eye
on the forest road,
a girl in a red sweatshirt.
I wave.
She waves back
and climbs up into
a mailbox.
She is sending herself
to see her grandmother.
Somewhere in childhood
a story of traveling through the woods
frightened her.
And so it is parcel post
is the safest way
for a girl to travel.

THE FUTURE

There goes the
Narcan truck

Toot toot to the
neighborhood kids

They're practicing
being soldiers

Hup two three four
I must admit

their martial instinct
is impressive

The way they line up
along the street

and wail like wolf pups
How they conceal

the swords of
undiscovered animosity

THE AGENDA

A car alarm activates the children of Glaze Court.
They flood out like a troop of gibbons,

howl in Slavic brogue and pick up sticks for guns,
not at all pleased with an encore pandemic summer.

The whole that should be happiness of youth
has Balkanized, and at dusk they beat trash cans

like tocsins and crush each other under stones.
In dim halo of streetlight they rough out the agenda.

Tomorrow we burn textbooks. And after,
we hot-wire adults to explode common decency.

ACCORDION PRACTICE

A waxing moon
charged by lithium.
The neighborhood hums
with pandemic
excitement of children
who've been furloughed
from the burdensome
responsibilities of fifth grade.
Down the street
either way they're singing
their own giddy versions
of ding dong
the witch is dead.
My children have grown silent.
Chloe has broken into
her turntable to find
the problem that plagues
the Beatles' Rubber Soul.
Henry has turned his room into a cave
the cats are afraid to enter.
He's going shirtless for good.
Someone's ringtone
goes on in the darkness
like a siren begging
for the sick and injured.
But no one will answer because
no one recognizes
the number of the Bureau
of Dyschronometria
and General Malaise.
We do not want to be

at this or any other end of a line.
If census workers show up now,
we'll say present and then
return to our accordion practice.

DAISIES FOR A CHAIN

The old woman
on Lofton Road
checks her mailbox
every afternoon.
The wind bends
tall grass.
Today she finds
a little girl inside.
Someone has sent
her daughter back
after so many years.
They walk up the
long gravel drive,
the old lady watching
the little girl pick
daisies for a chain.

BROTHERLY LOVE

The kid in the back
of the school bus

flips me off.
His head is illuminated

like Saint Ignatius
in my headlights.

Neither he nor I want
to be mobile at this hour.

When the bus jerks forward,
his face pounds the glass.

I laugh and flip him off.
He laughs and flips me off again,

and I follow him many miles
over dark passages of hills.

VULNERABLE BIRDS

The children from the house of dust
scurry out.

Quail that gather beneath the cedar trees
on St. John's Hill.

The school bus picks them up from an edge
of cloud hiding the forest.

In the fog they resemble humans in transition
to more vulnerable birds.

THE HEART OF THE SUN

The girl in cowboy boots
on Halls Hill Road
is destined to be abducted by aliens.
In fact, she welcomes a change.
I'm sick of banana trees
with no bananas
and the shitty cold sandwiches
at Neely's Market.
All the bad in life,
too much mayo,
and nothing for a girl to look forward to.
The aliens will probably be
full of shit,
halfhearted abductors,
and drop her off at Smith Hall
when she tries to set their controls
for the heart of the sun.

THE TRAGEDY OF GIRLS

Every Sunday in February
is quinceañera karaoke.
Girls are relinquishing tiaras
for work boots and aprons,
maternity pants.
The Mariachi band plays,
and sweat tastes like tears.
And the posole will
never taste the same.
Something added
or something taken away?
At midnight, a glitch
in the PA system sends
every dog howling.
Some dogs are young men
who've hung around
to see what happens next
despite the truck that
will pick them up
in four hours, drive them
to their smoldering sites.

DEFINE HAPPINESS

What of no school today
for the forest children

along Laura Thompson Trail?
Mrs. Jenkins has lost her mind.

What of Mrs. Jenkins
and her farmer husband?

What of the mess he's made
with their finances?

The eggs in one basket?
The prize billy picked over

by vultures on Hurricane Creek?
What of the shortfall hay?

No school today means
homework. Children,

pretend you have ten cows.
Give seven to the coyotes.

What of the remainder?
Do you sell them skinny

and hope to recoup
the cost of feeding the full ten

for a season? With your
calculators, divine the odds

of a marriage surviving
on a teacher's salary.

Now for your English lesson.
Define happiness.

LEOPARD

The foster girl two houses
down Kirkwood perfects
the art of warm weather squealing.
Though it's early March,
she knows now
to scream fire, wolf, cops.
At 65 degrees, she's
an air horn, and at bedtime
she sits in her bunk
purring like a leopard,
one eye open,
on the highest limb.

SATURDAY EVENING

The kids on Glaze Court
are throwing knives
against the house
and speaking the broken
code of ancient man.
Tomorrow the van will come
and try to lure them
to the Baptists, but for now
they resist the limitations
of a single fatherly god
for the gods of chaos
along the privet paths,
the gods of the living waters
of Lytle Creek with
their stone-faced idols
of the great overpass
and the stone and steel
gods of the railroad track
where they gather at dusk
to sacrifice pennies on
the long singing altars.

DREAMS

But the blue jay might not
prefer the role of villain.

As a child I found
a jay who'd been mocked

by crows and lost desire.
In robbing the nest

he swallowed something shiny.
That bird's sick, my dad said.

I put him in a shoebox,
plantain for bedding.

Buried him in rhubarb shade.
In the spring when people

turn soil with spades,
a featherless creature

made of bones.
And strung out along

the endless branch,
dreams.

JUBILEE

Today all talking ended on cue.
The last utterance was a mother
responding to her daughter.
A simple yes, dear.
No bombs exploded.
No anomalies in the spiral.
Decisions that were pending
were carried away by birds.
Horse-mouthed politicians
choked on their own spit.
The sound of coughing reverberated
throughout the Smithsonian.
Above the plain
sparrows brought down a fighter jet.
On the island
people watched silently
as turtles sank a gunship.
In the mountains
something old opened its eyes,
slipped into the dark channel.
On the playground
the young girl held one finger to her mouth
for a thousand years.

HAYDEN CARRUTH

Black ants who guard the sugars
of Mrs. Carruth's peonies
are appointed by the same gods
who smile upon naughty children
in Kentucky. My brother, sister and I
regularly mow Mrs. Carruth's yard.
She married a cousin of the poet
Hayden Carruth, and he says
our minds are the minds of men
who feel and imagine without time.
And so when I mow the lawn,
I say, the serenity of the present,
the repose of my eyes
in the cool whiteness of sterile flowers
leaves me wondering what's next?
The two dollars?
The drink of Kool-Aid?
The timeless touch of black soil
where peonies, unguarded,
droop amid standing stones
placed by the giant gods of ants
and children to whisper what is?
The earth a stretch of unruly grass
that catches our dreams
and keeps them moving, so resplendent?

ANYTHING BUT PHOEBE

The risk is naming your daughter
anything but Phoebe.

Name her Lark, and she'll fly
out the window in the dark.

Name her Wren, and she'll
never fly home again

but build a deceptive nest
in every other eave.

But Phoebe will go off to Mexico
for a season and return

a woman who no longer needs you
but just wants you to hear her

sing her name in the morning.
A fastidiousness and love.

The risk is naming your daughter
anything but Phoebe.

II.

FAIRYTALE

Do not forget before the war
a red fox crossed the road
in front of us, and we thought it
a normal morning occurrence.

But now we wonder where
was he off to in such a hurry?
Was he carrying the premonition?
Was he the premonition?

And what of the reality of a war?
A child's legs.
The old woman reading
Iron Age scriptures

as if their incantation
would make a difference.
The rubble of the old park
and koi left circling the pond.

What of the agitated crows
whose raucous reverberations
like hot wires extend from
an underground conduit

ready to provide the final shock?
And the dead grass
the fox disappeared through
like stage curtains?

Which creature makes
our story end
and the new story poised
with dark wings begin?

GREASY CHOPS

He pulled the curled corner
of wallpaper and uncovered
the soldiers huddled inside
the wall like sleeping roaches.

On cue, they advanced
through the village and killed
the weak and the old,
the young and all the lovers.

Behind the wall, too,
was a window, and beyond
the window a plain full
of people peering through.

Some were holding back
the others, and others were
putting on bibs and
licking their greasy chops.

BY THE HAIR

The Ukrainian lady slipped
on leaves and broke an ankle.

She waited, as is normal
for Ukrainians, for the bone

to heal before she called 911.
Five hours later a rescue arrived,

a nasty place in the back
of the woods by a dark seep.

She apologized for
inconveniencing the medics.

It's okay they said.
We're here to serve.

Even still, she responded,
you can drag me out by the hair.

YESTERDAY

The order comes down the line.
A child's game of whispering.
Shoot the hostages.

Yesterday I found a freshly dug hole
in the forest. Inside,
I saw where a mole

had extracted a cicada larva.
Left its head and legs
in a precious little pile.

COUNTERWEIGHT

All day the cuckoo.
Through the rain.
Through the fire.
The cicadas sing,
the smoke drifts.
People come in and out.
Someone cries from
behind a wall.
Over here! I'm suffering!
And someone else cries
from behind the same wall.
Over here! I'm suffering, too!
And all day the cuckoo,
and the cicada song
drifting like smoke.

I turn around and around
looking for the hitch,
a counterweight
larger and more expedient
than empathy
but find nothing satisfactory
to connect me to such misery.
If I had rope,
I could tie one end
around my neck
and throw the other end
over the wall.

ANOTHER 21ST CENTURY WAR

The toenail moon so calm
and full of spite
grandmothering the spoiled
cities of the south where
overgrown children demand more beer,
more St. Patrick's Day, more bike trails.

A million eyeballs illuminate
the darkness with science fiction.
Netflix has returned
to reclaim believers and reign
for a thousand years
of highly original, premium peace.

In the middle distance the sun pierces
a frosty stretch of farmland
where the tank commander cuts coffee
with gunpowder to spread it out
over miles of highway.

Today, he's told,
aim the cannon at the tree line,
where a defense of women
has amassed with spindles
disassembled from their own cribs.

HIGH BRIDGE, WINTER 1986

The day Roosevelt died
my old man puked on the floor
of the two-room shack.
Years later the Devil moved in.

Roosevelt is gone, his mother said,
and cried in her apron as
lard rendered in the pan,
eggshells burned to dust.

When I was sixteen, the Devil
passed out on the same floor,
drinking Eagle Rare dad insisted
for housewarming. Once upon

a January we cruised backroads
in a vain and necessary search
for the hard past. We ended there.
The two-room shack unaltered by

misery and joy. In the front,
generations of men toasting the
Devil to forget, and in the back,
ghosts of women unbound.

THANKSGIVING

The western front threatened all day.
A dark blanket at the foot of the bed.

The neighbor fussed over his smoker
expecting rain to ruin his plans.

The dog, about to be abandoned,
sensed a significant change in her status.

High above the earth a satellite recorded
the beginning of the new reality.

The dataset will not be analyzed
for a thousand years.

MEDIATORS

The debate over the size of the moon and whether
or not Orion is reckless with his bow

is settled by feral cats who screech
at passing motorcycles.

Stray dogs weigh in as well.
The moon is half-eaten, they howl.

Orion is dim enough to ignore.
Besides, the goal of these deliberations,

they say, is simply to keep neighbors
from killing one another over nonsense.

HIGHER EDUCATION

The only words left
in the old Liberty Schoolhouse
are written in spray paint.
Get fucked, Trevor.
Arithmetic has settled on a sum,
sold out and moved on.
The hard sciences remain
with no one to learn them.
The chemistry and physics
of decay behind a blackboard.
A curious little civics experiment
happens, though,
where the teacher's desk
has been replaced by a tree.
A quiet line of wood nymphs
climb up the bark
toward the higher education
of leaves.

THE WORK

The torturer had the perfect
morning commute.

Rain moved out,
and the clouds made

a sunrise inspired
by undiscovered gemstones.

In the forest pass
the deer seemed compliant,

willing somehow to return
to leaves.

He stopped to help
a turtle across the road.

The coffee tasted golden
and filled his spirit with light.

In this morning,
poised as it was

before the humdrum,
he could repeat

the simple song
of the wood thrush verbatim.

MOP

She was born blind
in a cold, damp chase
on third shift.

She inherited her
mother's long, thick hair,
all dirty blonde.

At school the teacher
made her stand in a corner
behind the door.

Two plus two is four.
A E I O U and
sometimes Y.

At night a spider
taught her to read braille,
and so she learned

the story of footsteps
and crumbs,
of spilt milk and sick.

A small grace,
some prudish mother said,
poor thing.

Suffer the children
to come unto me
was her favorite bit of scripture.

To them belongs
the kingdom of heaven
she would sing

as she dragged
herself across
the nighttime floors.

DOMICILE

Only now that I'm dying,
I need a simple truth.

There in the kitchen corner,
rough shock frazzled,

the patina of a handle,
the sweat of a palm.

How we danced our lives away
in the secret of four walls.

Showed out what came in
to gather unwanted.

Were you counting days
from dust to dust as I was?

To what end and for whose
love did you toil, sister?

MOP BUCKET

Everyone assumed he
was just a natural
at carrying water.

Flawless, he thought.
He was king
of the chase.

A man with a reliable
set of hard
plastic wheels.

But one day he failed.
Split his wringer,
cracked down the side.

An unseen
weakness in his
manufacture.

The water got out
and would never
stay in again.

So they rolled him
out back
and chucked him

in the dumpster
as if he'd never done
anything right.

Each night for a week
he dreamed only
of the one failure

until it defined
his entire life
like a hieroglyph

acid-etched in some
cold, filthy
kitchen tile.

So when the man came
to collect the trash,
he quietly followed.

DUST

The broom shop closed
early this season.

The broom-maker
driven off by the plague.

Brooms that did not sell
hang on the wall.

Why aren't we all
beatified? they whisper.

What despairs more
than god's idle hand?

Between them,
the negative space

of someone who
would be industrious.

While under the table,
a place to settle the argument.

DUST PAN

On the first day of school
the dust pan realized he had

a monstrous underbite.
The other children taunted him

with chants of slack jaw freak.
When the teacher asked him

for a diphthong, the tiny voice
in his handle said no.

At recess he crossed the fence
and ran away. He tried to fly

but landed flat in the road
and cried for hours.

He counted out the pebbles
and spelled the names

of things he knew. I am not
some stupid animal on a leash.

But when the broom
found him, she took him back

to the schoolhouse and fed him
his dinner on the floor.

HAPPINESS

The broom left god's workshop
with many novel ideas about

the nature of industry and soon
found forced labor in Alabama.

Nobody likes a complaining broom,
they said. Nor a broom that speaks

out of turn. Nor a broom that makes
eye contact. Certainly not a broom

that reads Marx before the good
book. So she swept under the rug.

Her existence, it seemed, hinged
upon her ability to marshal dust.

Her mother was the archangel
Evangeline, the messenger

of good news. Why did god need
to kill a son, the broom wondered,

to bring the good news? I am
my mother's daughter.

Let me tell the nations
what is next to cleanliness.

For this insubordination,
god thought, the broom

will be bound to dust.
You will sweep, he proclaimed

through puffs of his pipe,
eternity and never find happiness.

So the broom swept, and
in her seemingly mindless tasks,

she found happiness
to dignify all honest work

despite the almighty proclamations
of god, and so transmitted

to the hands of the least
among us their immense value.

PENITENT FRIEND

The broom-maker built a house
from sassafras for his creations.

He moved to the garage
with the Harley Davidson.

He still loved her even though
she only idled about.

His children contracted the plague,
quarantined in Memphis.

His girlfriend bought a camper
and set out for the Grand Canyon.

He told the radio he was lonely,
grew darker, and let himself go

like an old slice of apple
fallen behind the banquette

where he welcomed dust
as an old penitent friend.

ANECDOTES FOR THE BROOM

1.

A life spent in sooty caves.
Neanderthal dreamed

an antidote to filth and turned
a spear into a broom.

Among the pantheon
of spirit animals,

the inverted spear
represents the first domestic

weapon and takes precedence
even above the basket.

2.

On the day he would die,
Publius Quinctilius Varus carried

a small ivory-handled broom
among his armaments

into the Teutoburg Forest,
a totem that later found

its way to Bohemia and
the Marcomanni longhouse

of King Marbod
where it was used to

exorcize mouse turds
from the royal granary.

Recovered along with
the last of the legion's eagles

in 42 AD, the broom
returned to Rome

to be honored as consul
of the empire's little dirty places.

3.

Though we remember
her name synonymous

with hatchet,
Carrie Nation's first

weapon was the long-handled
Kentucky broom.

Its violence, though, did not
jar the social conscience,

so she adopted the hatchet
and vowed to make

rather than clean
a mess with it.

4.

When the broom-maker-god
approaches, do not despair.

Go with him to the little shop
where straw and twine are dyeing.

You are dying he'll say
and cinch the wire.

He's binding you
to a hickory handle

so you can see all problems,
all conflagrations,

great or small, within and
without, for what they

truly are: mere dust.
Of no cosmic import.

As a broom, you will know
intuitively what must be done.

THE MEASURE

The next time we meet
I'll be transitioning
into a measuring tape.
All I've ever wanted
was to provide some accuracy.
Maybe you'll be delighted
at the full extent
or disappointed at
the shortcoming.
Whichever occurs to you,
I'll retract on myself.
You can pull me apart
more quickly then,
see my segments,
the fractions I embody.
You just say what you need.
I'll lie down flat against it
so you can make your mark
and cut away the scrap.

III.

TWO CROWS

Two crows converge on a puddle
to discuss local politics.

See the frog? one asks.
The other grabs it in his beak.

Then the first crow grabs
a dangling leg. They wrestle.

The frog has no agency
and thrashes hopelessly.

They want an equitable
distribution of resources,

but their mouths are
too full to enunciate the words,

and soon their bellies are full
of frog, and they forget equality.

TOWHEE

The ground robin arrives to unlock
dead faces inside the garden.

The key, a single seed of coneflower.
His black hood and tawny shawl

sit me up in a dream of blue stars,
poor health and numbered days,

like an executioner who brings flowers
to work and cries over his lunch

at what must be done
in the evening.

ALL THE ANIMALS MADE GOOD DECISIONS

All the animals made
good decisions today
except for the human.

The young rabbit
wisely hopped off
into the plantain

along the roadside
and did not panic
into oncoming traffic.

The kingbird chasing
the grasshopper
broke off pursuit,

returned to his wire,
the road too dangerous,
and flashed a white flag.

But the human woke up,
continued in his normal
course of habits,

running into the onslaught
that doesn't kill him
instantaneously, but

over time, as if vision
was perfect and he could look
beyond his moment.

CATBIRD

Today I wait on a single word
unknown to me that I open with

my mouth and pass through
like a cedar bough.

Where the utterance ends
I perch because

I am going to die but
can't yet appreciate it.

Birds have always understood
this migration as imperative.

Take the catbird
practicing her medicine.

The hoarse meeurrs
and cackling kedekekeks.

The deep whurfs, all
signaling a life at once glorious

on the highest branch
then gone beneath the hedge.

DIG HERE

A downy unravels
a tree.

Find out where
to begin your puzzle.

Goldenrod bronzed
and grey.

Two bluebirds gone
through a knot.

I'm so good at piling
pieces that don't fit,

wood, stone.
A quail middles the earth.

Wood and stone
off to the side.

A feather of doubt
singing

is anyone at home
with what they've done?

MID-DAY

The lacewing takes its place
beneath St. John's leaf,

and I sit beneath a tree
of heaven.

We wait out the hottest hour,
contemplating

hopelessness that gains
on all sides

then fly off in opposite directions
toward oblivion.

THE EFFECT

The male bunting rehearses
the mellifluous cadence of sex,

reflecting brilliant blue
in quivering heat.

One hundred notes.
But when he flits to shadow

beneath the cane,
he becomes a shadow too,

not at all certain, and wonders
is there no end to madness?

UNDERSTORY

Show up to work early just to
hear the birds at rock bottom.

Two notes repeated
go on till daylight. Phoebes.

At the point where their song
ends the day begins,

hollow at first,
then filling with hope.

Clean nest, clean nest,
they say and drop their shit

in the tidy dark
understory.

TURN OF A SEASON

Reliable as memory of spring,
wood thrush, what will happen next?
When will the good times run out?

How you have come so far
with the same simple song,
swallowing anxiety and fear

like a little green caterpillar.

CREEKSIDE TABLEAU

If it weren't rooted,
bees would carry

the buckeye away,
each bloom a tower

of hyperactivity.
The lowest branches

bow to receive the
sacraments of pollination.

In the shade Iodanthus
wakes from sleep,

its many eyes
exploding with light.

THE FUTURE AGAIN

The future shines
bright before us

like the harvest moon
reflected in the

bottom of a septic tank.
To get there, we'll have

to get by on less,
stomach a foul

march through
the mess we've made.

JOB OPENING

Darkness at the forest edge.
Edwards Hill, the mourning

dove, the quail,
the speckled rump

of the American robin.
Between two ashes,

an opening for assistant curator
of forest murmurings.

How do you feel about
working the dark edge?

And brown thrashers?
You must be able to

leave the road quickly
and carry obligations

through the geography
of morning spiders.

The pay's not at all sufficient.
But the benefits

include disappearing
for long periods,

discovering what to say
with no one to say it to.

CINCINNATI ARCH

When it comes to pressure
and time, this place is diamond.

I've lived most of my allotment
between limestone ledges.

Grown some killer dope
where the railroad ground through.

Pulled out a cephalopod
as long as my arm.

Plowed up my father's wallet
ten years after he'd plowed it under.

One decrepit sawbuck.
A driver's license.

One end of my time
trifolding back to the other.

ANOTHER PANDEMIC DISPATCH

Ten months in, infection
and death spiking,

I climb on the porch
of the writing shack

to take in the armageddon
of my neighbor's yard.

Looks like a sporting
goods store fell off

the back of a truck.
The trampoline leans a little,

and on one side a small pool
of green water gathers.

Nascent frog material.
Balls of all sizes wait

in tall grass for kids
who abandoned them.

Bats, a cheap little
catcher's mitt,

some plastic ends detached
from plastic beginnings.

Where do the children play?
I hum to myself.

Dead banana leaves rustle
in November wind,

but a week of 80 degree
weather has the Jessamine vine

all beset with flower buds.
Some of them are trying to open.

Everywhere it seems innate
behavioral mechanisms

are being rewired
for self-destruction.

XERIC ENVIRONMENTS

Blue chip has always been my signifier
according to the retirement plan.

Its update reads me like a book
about someone else.

I peruse the summary listening
to Benny Goodman while sipping

honey liqueur. The investment
objective is growth,

and shareholder fees are fed
upon this growth.

I can't help but wonder how much they've
grown along with operating expenses

while a squirrel outside the window
motions with his head

at another squirrel who's trundling
a walnut into the forsythia.

Another sip of liqueur.
I chase my tail four times in a circle.

Sentences in the Liquidity Risk Management
read like liquid Xanex.

Martha Tilton sings I must see
Annie tonight.

I must find a way to work
the term illiquid

into some routine
about xeric environments.

ERRANT MEANDER

Just enough snow to cover
the deadfall.

We made it this far
unexalted by sun.

A kingfisher guards
Fall Creek,

peering at a hole
in the ice

and the old routes
of fish.

Every winter has
changed us.

This winter just seems
deeper at the start.

I touch my face
like a cartographer

reviewing his work
and find

hard miles of
errant meander.

PRESENT

In the red peanut glow
of Christmas décor I awaken

from a musical dream
where I lead tours through

the ground robin's castle.
I drink his tea. In the darkness

of the hill a lost dog groans.
When my eyes wake up,

I call out which song is that?
and the voice answers

it's your song. This is the
emergency room, the ancient tat

angel bending slowly to break
the news, you are dead but

you are not completely
alone yet. My children

behind the next curtain
make beaded jewelry

and speak in low friendly voices.
I hear the happy sound

of gentle people leaving
on wooden snowshoes.

They have left me beneath
the tree where time has come,

and in the morning the bird
will fly down and open me.

IV.

CEREMONY

In the cool morning
the homeless gather
on the pauper cemetery
near Lytle Creek
to celebrate another equinox.
Following a brief prayer
to the sun god,
a symbolic offering of
the lady who froze to death,
the worn-out shoes,
the soiled sweatpants,
the ratty coat
with the broken zipper.
And the main event,
a grand feast of dreams.
The short woman with
long hair eats a dream
of a cozy trailer home
with clean carpet,
pinging baseboard heaters,
and a toilet that flushes.
The teenage boy with
the sore tooth
eats a soft dream
of new wool socks and
a plush recliner.
And not to be outdone,
the dreamless man
who pushes the Target
shopping cart through
a waking nightmare,
holds an empty soup can
to his ear,

eats the sound of ocean
repeating itself,
and offers the double
amputee a helping
of warm sand
to feel between his toes.

SUMMER SOLSTICE

The dead rise from
the pauper cemetery

disguised as goldenrod
and ironweed

beneath the shadow
of Pluck Miller bridge.

The man covered
in sweat bees,

a filthy drunk
who bankrupted his family

at the racetrack,
shines like the queen of all nature

and throws wind
around him like a cape.

The murderer and
the murdered dance

in the wind,
one stretching over the other

without menace
to ask who's the monster now?

When they were
just homeless mates,

they fought over
an energy drink.

The woman who walked
in front of the train

when Child Services
confiscated her daughter

dances alone,
bends to ask the daisy,

does this bumblebee
make my ass look big?

WINTER SCENARIO IN AMERICA

Current cracks under
the ice on Lytle Creek

and the train screams
its icy rails.

A vulture, just in from
metro Atlanta,

roosts on a privacy fence,
all pithed and

given up on
exalting the dead.

The clouds move as
reluctantly as justice.

The old vet in the sweat jacket
stops to size up

a heap of scrap metal
for tonight's coffin.

His snow angel looks
like a dead dog.

INCARCERATION

In General Population
orange jumpsuits line up
for breakfast.
This morning's serving,
your wildest dreams.
Some eat guns,
others eat knives,
but most eat their drug
of choice.
The old man on the cot
eats cigarettes and whiskey,
the kitchen table and chair
where he sat down
after he'd done what he'd done,
the doorway where
the children hid in the dark.

SHADOW DOCKET

A tiny sound bothers Amy during
a dream of pope Benedict XVI.

He's tinking his tiny triangle.
She wakes, a vampire's bride.

Yes, master, she mutters,
throwing another Atwood

in the stove
to warm the ferrets.

The Supreme Court is
hearing Mississippi today,

for its desire to reroute
Fallopian tubes toward the Bible.

She finishes her melba toast,
grabs her robe and kibosh

and starts up her dragon.
Today is a good day

to say one thing
and do another.

THE GOOD LIFE

The people who lived here
killed themselves with industry.

Note the chinking between joints,
the backbone recurved

like a Vegas trick.
French archeologists make

parallels.
Neanderthal bones exhibit

similar pressures.
The life of bending in and out

of tight places,
the seasonal hoppossing

and fuss over household
valuables, like the one good spoon,

the stir stick, the hammer stone,
all the fucking hides, the poles,

combined with the worry
of strangers passing,

the rheumatic ice age nights
caught in the damp.

Compare this femur with
its stress lines. This individual

fell into a deep depression
and was trampled by god

only knows but got up and
rejoined the effort

of whatever they
were laboring toward,

a mad man in every direction
promising the good life.

THE GREAT MISTAKE

When all the gods
were animals,
the sacrament
was survival.
It was easier
to believe.
And more believable
than textual myth.
Paleolithic humans
could carry
the gods inside
their bellies,
wear them on
their backs during
spring migrations,
paint them in caves
for posterity,
and leave the outline
of their hands
as testament.
The great mistake
happened when
the image of hands
became god.

50TH BIRTHDAY

The world is a breast-
shaped stone occupied
by mockingbirds and idiots.
This pocket is home
to an idiot.
His name is Wes.

When jets come
out of supersonic rage
and begin their descent
towards Nashville,
I always look up
expecting the tail
to break off like a skink.

Looking up
is one way to
nurture idiocy.

The other way
is to talk to animals
and wait for reply.
The spiny softshell turtle
in Lytle Creek as big
as a garbage can lid
says stones have a current.
Maintain steady pace.

The stone that will
name you after you're gone
is already migrating
toward its chisel.

LOCKSMITHING

A house finch concusses
the window on a stone cabin.
He asks, who doesn't
like ice cream with their
birthday cake?

The finch has three
main segments:
A crown, a wing, a hand.
If he compresses
the tiny spring inside his core,
he might stay finch forever.

Today all my segments
equal fifty-two.
That's eleven finch lives
laid end to end.
Between my observing
a finch and taking action,

a shear line matching
a landscape of scars.
The murmur of tiny springs.
I have turned a skeleton key
fifty-two times.
I haven't died once.

PAX ROMANA

My face is composed of the
uneasy alliance of many European

tribal states that exist now only
in obscure books and my face.

Maybe it's your face, too.
The geology of barbarians.

Dark forests used to cover the
ground. Not so much now,

but a certain hapless scrunch
of the brow that says so

much about duplicity of future
crimes. Barrows mark me.

One on my ear, in western
Germany. Rhine country.

A chieftain's burial with a wife.
Perhaps a dog. A favorite cup.

Each morning a part of the face
that pays Caesar for keeping

peace in the forested north
looks back at me in disgust.

THE MONTH BEFORE SOLSTICE

At the bottom of the river,
Orconectes placidus
polishing a piece of quartz.

In the path of the
celestial plane, a flint point
discarded by the ancients.

A woman with blue hair
sketching a long weekend
smiles hello.

She's also writing a poem
about the rattlesnake master
in full bloom.

My friend and I stumble along,
drunk and leaning,
to keep pace with beautiful women.

COMMUNITY

The old lady across the street
has never liked me,
but I go to her yard sale anyway.

Her tastes are impeccably
shitty, eighth decade,
20th century.

A JC Penny's couture
which outfits every
mother and sister of memory.

A button attachment for
an antique Singer sewing machine.
I'll give you a dollar.

That's worth at least five,
she says. I remember why
she doesn't like me.

Over a decade ago I told her
she'd better pick up
her yappy little dog's shit

from my yard or by god
I'd put it in her mailbox.
Chloe wants the mirror

leaning against a tree.
I snarl at the full,
ugly extent of myself.

7/16^{THS}

If there are sixteen,
then seven belong to god
and the carpenter bee.
The sacred fraction,
seven-sixteenths.
Its wrench looks like
a tool for adjusting your
great-aunt's toes.
Measure your toes
to see if you are worthy.

The black hole at the center
of the Milky Way seems
enormous.
Four million suns, they say.
But it's seven-sixteenths
sure as shit.
Sure as spring.
The guy eating the donut
has crossed the
event horizon.

The corpse may protest,
but they will dig
the hole at seven-sixteenths.
The man smoking the cigarette,
hand gesturing to
the excavator doesn't
know why.
Death rearranges sixteenths
for the living.

And if your cross
is made of wood

and filled with every
déjà vu,
the carpenter bee
will wake you
when the good souls rise
and say
I've made you this peephole.

SALT AND ICE

Today was the perfect day
for resurrecting the dead.

In dreams, in dust,
sweeping them into ourselves,

swallowing them in great
gulps of stratosphere,

sifting them from
darkness and holding

their bodies in the baleen,
telling them the story

of since they were gone
in the middle language

we learned when our mouths
were full of salt and ice.

SO MUCH OF A MAP IS UNREADABLE

So many hills without names.
This one with the tipped-over shingle oak,

and that one where cedars
swallowed the Clemons' place.

Do we name them for what
went down: windstorm,

lightning strike,
gut-shot deer, brucellosis?

Do we call them out for what
they're not: the hill that's not

the steep one, the one that's not
where the Buick died?

Over which hill do we travel
through woods to grandma's house?

So much of a map is unreadable.

A barred owl kings
the next hill in February,

cries mid-mornings,
the air just cold enough and dark.

Then for as long as something
listens, the name

for this hill is the sad
sad song of days.

ANOTHER GLADELARKING

Whippoorwill glade margins
jeweled with late summer gumweed.

Rose pink hanging on.
A gold finch burns in atmosphere.

At the far end a single
branch of persimmon waves.

My father waved like that
across the tobacco field

so many years ago.
No great effort,

just an arm raised momentarily
to say let's go home.

Something similar
is about to happen

in the next universe,
and I want to be there.

NORWEGIAN TROLLS

Neanderthal shamans ponder
the origin of hummingbirds.

They are either descended from
the small rhino people or insects

that long ago molested volcanoes.
The ability to fly backwards

is indeed strange magic, though.
But they are not fledged of mud.

Only the phoebe and the cliff
swallow followed that course.

They came from dragons.
There once existed a pact

among proto-humans that we
would not desecrate birds

because of their small stature,
potbellied with shamefully

skinny legs, but so much of
their appearance was due to

unorthodox diets. When they
taught us to eat seeds and

suckle flowers with our noses,
so much of our beastliness

disappeared. We shaved ourselves.
Attempted to look more birdlike.

But evolution is a heartless
boss. We never mastered flight.

Not in the cards, heavy bones.
We have difficulty even walking

backwards for any distance
while muttering oaths or prayers.

If we could train our hearts
to crackle with the tiny fire

of hummingbirds, our anxieties,
so amplified, would turn us

to stone from the inside out
just like Norwegian trolls.

SISYPHUS

What is left of the stone
I've been pushing
is mainly calcium carbonate,
iron oxide,
the pitch of my palms.
Barely enough salt
to catch a falling angel.
That this difficult
proposition stalls me
would be cause for laughter
were it not for realization
the stone is actually pulling
me under its tread.
And besides, each laugh
would just acknowledge
my complicity with ignorance.

AFTER THE PROTESTS

The police helicopter kept me up
all night,
doing its rough figure eights
endlessly over downtown,
a droning thwack thwack
punctuated now and again
by an officer on a bullhorn
yelling now listen people.

Today I take my lunch
into the hardwoods.
Across the road,
Edwards Hill slopes up
somewhere through a broad
strait of motionless climax
hickory, oak, ash
where only weebirds stir
the air.
They end their songs
with resignation to some
great, overwhelming reality
about life
but go on living.

A raincrow repeats its plaintive refrain
to no one.
It tries the hollow, joyless laugh.
Still nothing.
A fox kit barks for its mother.
If the world tilts one degree,
every unfound object of affection
will slide away for good.
And there is a deep rumbling.

Back in town,
the newly bedded impatiens
at the intersection of X and Y
are jaundiced with tear gas.

DREAM VACATION

We are on a dream vacation,
skiing down the
it does not Matterhorn.
Boy, it's rocky.
And there isn't any snow.
We don't know how to ski.
We don't actually have
skis on our feet.
We are just falling down,
end over end.
I bang my head twice.
You scratch your bottom.
Back at the lodge,
they're hoisting whiskey drinks
in our honor.
The stone fireplace
is exquisite.
The bear rug, too.
Did we die?
Who are they
to commemorate
our short lives with whiskey?
Why did we do
what we did?
I wonder what is being mentioned.
Will they toast
our less foolish times,
or will we go down
like Jack and Jill
as the fire turns to coals
and the guests

retire to their suites,
laughter
still on their faces?

ABOUT THE AUTHOR

Wesley Houp was born and raised in High Bridge and Wilmore, Kentucky. He received a PhD in Composition and Rhetoric from Indiana University of Pennsylvania and taught undergraduate and graduate English courses for over 20 years in Kentucky, Pennsylvania and Tennessee in addition to serving as Writing Center Director at several universities. For the better part of the last decade, he has worked for Tennessee State Parks. His poems have appeared in numerous journals, including *Black Warrior Review, Chattahoochee Review, Kentucky Poetry Review,* and *Good River Review.* His scholarly work in literacy education and pedagogy has appeared in *Journal of Adolescent and Adult Literacy* and *Teaching English in the Two-Year College,* among others. This volume, his first, won the inaugural James Baker Hall Book Award for Poetry in 2024. He currently lives in Murfreesboro, Tennessee with his wife, Laura and their daughter and son, Chloe and Henry.